Railways around Manchester

Compiled by John Glover
Images from the Transport Treasury Library

The
· The ·
Transport
Treasury

The Transport Treasury

Reviving the memories of yesterday…

© Images and design: The Transport Treasury 2022. Text John Glover.

ISBN 978-1-913251-38-3

First published in 2022 by Transport Treasury Publishing Ltd., 16 Highworth Close, High Wycombe, HP13 7PJ

www.ttpublishing.co.uk

Printed in the UK by Henry Ling Limited at the Dorset Press, Dorchester, DT1 1HD

Front Cover: No. 42589 was a Stanier 2-cylinder Class 4 2-6-4T of 1935, calling at what are now Salford Central platforms on 21 August 1964. This is a stopping passenger train and the top lamp bracket on the smokebox door has been moved down and to the right. A later change and as a consequence of 25kV ac overhead electrification, this was to keep the enginemen safe by avoiding the need to reach as high as the former central position, with its proximity to the increasingly commonplace electrification equipment. *FM32-1 - Larry Fullwood*

Frontispiece: This is the external view of the station building on Manchester's Liverpool Road. The 31 miles of railway connecting it to Liverpool opened on 17 September 1830, though its use as a passenger terminal continued only until 4 May 1844. From then, its trains used the Manchester Victoria terminal, opened earlier that year. Liverpool Road's use was then confined to goods traffic and this shows the entrance to the General Offices of the Goods Department in British Railways days. It continued in limited use until as late as 1975; this photograph was taken on 12 May 1956. The station is now part of the Manchester Museum of Science and Industry. *AEB1185 - A.E Bennett*

Back Cover: After six years work in construction, the Ship Canal was opened by Queen Victoria on 21 May 1894. At 36 miles, it is still the longest river navigation in the world. More than 54 million cubic yards of material were excavated; the canal depth is now 28ft, maximum boat length is (nominally) 600ft and width 65ft 6in. There are five locks. In this view, an MSC-owned Hudswell Clarke 0-6-0ST is seen shunting. This was the long tank version, one of 20 in the fleet. Carrying more water gave the locomotive the ability to travel rather further before it needed to visit more water supplies, however far away that they might be. *23318 - Photographer Unknown*

Contents

This plaque was attached above the entrance to the offices of the Liverpool & Manchester Railway by the Lord Mayor of Liverpool, Lawrence Durang Holt, and the Lord Mayor of Manchester, Robert Noton Barclay, on 15 September 1930. This was to mark the centenary of the first public railway serving Manchester's first station. *AEB1186 - A.E Bennett*

Introduction

This book illustrates the railways of Greater Manchester as they were in the latter part of the twentieth century. The period covered is roughly the 40 years following nationalisation in 1948. In terms of major stations, this includes Manchester Piccadilly (formerly London Road), Manchester Victoria (before the major rebuilding) and Manchester Oxford Road (during and post reconstruction around 1960). Also covered are the now closed Manchester Central (which became G-Mex but is once again Manchester Central (Exhibition Centre) and Manchester Exchange (demolished). Pride of place is given to the original but still extant 1830 terminus of Liverpool Road. This is now part of Manchester's Museum of Science+Industry.

The book sections start with Liverpool Road in the middle of the city. Next are the Great Central's Woodhead route and, proceeding clockwise, followed by the London & North Western lines towards Stockport and beyond, the Manchester, South Junction & Altrincham Railway, and the Midland Railway towards Derby. Following is that consortium which challenged the dominance of London & North Western and Lancashire & Yorkshire interests in the area, known as the Cheshire Lines Committee. Then there is the London & North Western Railway's Manchester Exchange station, the Lancashire & Yorkshire lines towards Wigan (and a quick look at the West Coast Main Line), Bolton and then the Bury electrics. These are followed with the Lancashire & Yorkshire lines at Newton Heath, around Oldham and then on to Rochdale. Final parts include a section on Manchester Victoria, the London & North Western towards Stalybridge and Saddleworth and the now defunct Manchester Ship Canal Railway.

The heritage sector has not been included as such; the emphasis is on the railway as it was in the years concerned, with occasional updates in the text. A selection of rail tours has also been found a place.

My thanks are due to those who supplied the original images and the time they spent in getting them. All pre-date the advent of Manchester Metrolink, the first stage of which, linking Bury with Altrincham, was opened by HM The Queen on 17 July 1992.

In compiling this book, the author has tried to present a fair overview of the railways in the Manchester area, defined as that of the Greater Manchester authority plus a few extras on the fringes. All the photographs are sourced from the files of The Transport Treasury; many were well annotated, but the details could be rather lacking. The key questions that normally require answering are What? Where? and When? Some of the lines pictured are now defunct, let alone the trains which are seen using them. Other scenes have changed out of all recognition. He has been able to fill many gaps from his own knowledge, or by research (see the list of references). Dates are the most difficult to get right. He hopes that he has been reasonably successful, but also that readers will forgive any errors or omissions they may detect.

John Glover
Worcester Park, Surrey
February 2022

The ex-Lancashire & Yorkshire Railway (L&Y) 0-6-0 no. 52348 has arrived at Liverpool Road station on the Liverpool & Manchester on 12 May 1956 with the 'Old Manchester Tour' for both the Stephenson and the Manchester Locomotive Societies. The platform used for departing passengers, well below present heights, is to the left of the picture, but the arrival platform was the far side of the bridge over Water Street. It will be noted that the 1956 passengers had to make do with portable steps. The goods platform is to the right, occupied by a selection of covered goods vans. *AEB1188 - A.E Bennett*

No. 52348 demonstrates how hardy the enginemen of the day had to be with a cab so open to the elements. There were more than 200 members of this class of 0-6-0s, power classification 3F. They were introduced by the Lancashire & Yorkshire Railway's Chief Mechanical Engineer, John A F Aspinall, in 1899. This was 12 May 1956, so the then surviving class members had already been in traffic for half a century. There is no longer any railway connection to the national network. *AEB1187 A. E. Bennett*

This is the Liverpool & Manchester railway bridge at the end of Liverpool Road at its junction with Water Street. The arrival platform was to the left of the bridge, departures to the right. It is the background for a number of advertisements, 12 May 1956 vintage. These include 'Beer is the best long drink in the world', 'He's a Mackeson type and all the better for it' and 'Have a Wall's, Good and Big'. There are directions to 'A Bromage & Son, Briar Pipe Manufacturers and Repairers', while you are reminded about the 'Makers of Slaters superior pork sausages'. *AEB1184 - A.E Bennett*

The Woodhead Route

The low numbered platforms at Manchester Piccadilly were used by the former Manchester, Sheffield & Lincolnshire (Great Central from 1899) services. Here, Class EM2 Co-Co no. 27005 *Minerva,* built in 1954, waits at Platform 1 with a service for Penistone and Sheffield. These locomotives were built for passenger (as opposed to the goods) services, and were provided with six traction motors. These had a rating of 2,490hp. In the event, their higher power rating over the EM1 was found to be unnecessary. On 5 October 1968 the whole class was withdrawn and sent for storage in the former steam shed at Bury. In Autumn 1969 they were exported for use by Netherlands Railways as their new owner. *SJH (3) - Stephen Hoather*

Here, on 22 July 1968, Manchester Piccadilly sees Class EM1 Bo-Bo no. 26056 *Triton* with a service for Sheffield Victoria. These 1,500v dc locomotives had four traction motors and were rated at 1,868hp. The original class member (BR no. 26000) was built in 1940, and loaned to Netherlands Railways after the end of WW2 to assist their reconstruction. It was there that it acquired its name *Tommy.* Further production of EM1s did not proceed until the post-war era. With some minor changes, building recommenced in 1950, but full operations had to wait for the completion of the new Woodhead tunnel in 1954. *AS Y23-3 - Alec Swain*

Opposite Top: Manchester Piccadilly's Platform 3 in August 1968 sees Driving Trailer Open Second no. M59603M with a local service departure on the 1,500v dc lines to Hadfield. These 3-car units with sliding doors were basically similar to those built earlier for the Liverpool Street-Shenfield electrification, but eight sets only were considered sufficient for the Glossop/Hadfield services, as opposed to 92 for Shenfield. The latter were later converted for use on ac electrification, but the dc Manchester units were scrapped and replaced (for a time) by trains from the Glasgow system. *AS Y33-3 - Alec Swain*

Opposite Bottom: No. M59402M was a Driving Motor Open Brake Third when built, later Second. It was photographed here on 14 June 1961 having just left Manchester Piccadilly at the rear of a six-car train for Hadfield. The oil tail lamp on the rear will be noted. A physical tail lamp was to be something which would remain a safety requirement for many more years. A train without a tail lamp is not complete, and signalmen needed to act accordingly. *AHR - Alan Roscoe*

Above: As many as 732 of the War Department's (WD) 2-8-0s were taken into the newly formed British Railways stocklist on nationalisation in 1948 and were deployed wherever BR considered them suitable. They were, in effect, an economy version of the Stanier 2-8-0s for the LMS, which had proved very successful. Known to enthusiasts as 'Dub Ds', no. 90671 is undergoing a crew change at Ashburys on 21 March 1960. These locomotives disappeared gradually from view, and few, it would seem, mourned their passing. The British Railways Standard 9F was an altogether superior beast, but the first of those and also the last of the Standard classes did not appear until 1954. *AS H22-3 - Alec Swain*

The Class O1 of which no. 63590 was an example were 1944 rebuilds by Edward Thompson for the LNER of the Class O4 2-8-0 group of locomotives and their many variations. The design could be traced back to that by J G Robinson for the Great Central Railway, who was in charge of such matters from 1900 to 1922. No 63590 was seen at Ashburys on 21 March 1960. *AS H22-2 - Alec Swain*

The workhorses of the Manchester-Sheffield-Wath electrification were to be the 57 EM1 locomotives nos. 26000 to no. 26057, later Class 76. They were built by British Railways in Doncaster from 1950, a former London & North Eastern Railway stronghold. No. 26002 is at Gorton in 1959, newly painted in express passenger green and lined out. Not bad for a machine whose primary use was intended to be for freight. *NS208040 - Neville Stead*

No. 62301 was a Great Central Railway Class D9 4-4-0 built in 1901. It is seen here in October 1949 with its front end lifted and suspended from a hoist. This was sufficient for the bogie to be removed. The rear driving wheels, only, remained on the rails. Latterly a Trafford Park locomotive, it was withdrawn from service in April 1950 and cut up two months later. *REV97A-2-4 - Roy Vincent*

Above: This C14 4-4-2T no. 67450 was photographed at Guide Bridge station in 1954 on a local service. Steam locomotives need copious supplies of water to create the steam and hence drive the train along. Water cranes were frequently to be found at the larger stations, where a longer stop would be needed to replenish the tanks. Notable here is the receptacle for the sleeve, aimed no doubt at preventing the platform from being flooded from time to time. *NS202700 - Neville Stead*

Opposite Top: Tank locomotives of a Pacific wheel arrangement were decidedly rare in Britain, but the Great Central A5 class 4-6-2T's of J G Robinson were hefty 86 ton examples. No. 69806 was built in 1911, and this class which extended to 43 locomotives formed a notable exception. This photograph of a local service at Guide Bridge was taken in 1958. *NS202665 - Neville Stead*

Opposite Bottom: Dinting station of 1847 had two platforms on the main Manchester Sheffield double track line (behind the camera), and again on the branch from the Manchester direction to Glossop. This view of 27 April 1960 shows the up branch platform for trains from Glossop towards Manchester. With the subsequent single tracking (of the whole branch), this platform is not now used, so trains no longer call there. *AS H63-6 - Alec Swain*

No. M59604M was a Driving Trailing Second of what was known latterly as Class 506 for the 1.500v dc line to Glossop and Hadfield. It is seen here leaving Dinting for Manchester Piccadilly. These LNER designed units were built in 1950, but it was some years before they entered service. They had what was to become a standard approach for short distance suburban services, of two pairs of sliding doors on each side of each vehicle and saloon seating within. They were not gangwayed between vehicles. *No record*

The shed at Dinting sees Fowler 4F no. 44025 of 1911 for the Midland Railway idling its time away. A total of over 600 of this and another design developed from it were built for the Midland and its London, Midland & Scottish Railway successor. It is accompanied by a line of less than pristine looking 16t mineral wagons, which one presumes had brought in coal supplies for the shed. *AS H63-5 - Alec Swain*

The town of Glossop was served by a dead end branch from Dinting, with the track laid out so that trains could reverse at Glossop and then continue towards Hadfield, the present terminus, but not via Dinting on this movement. The station was renamed Glossop Central in 1922 and is seen here with that name on 27 April 1960. It reverted to plain Glossop in 1974. The present platform of what is now a single track terminal branch, without sidings, has been rerouted to the other side of that shown here.
AS H63-3 - Alec Swain

The pair of single track Woodhead tunnels through the Pennines on the Manchester, Sheffield & Lincolnshire route were seen here very much out of use, with the track removed. The new Woodhead tunnel, right, was opened in 1954, and with it the repositioned Woodhead station platforms. Woodhead station, and hence the platforms, was closed a mere decade later on 27 July 1964. Even a quick look around the area makes one wonder where the passenger traffic was expected to come from. But this was primarily a freight railway, and the principal traffic was coal across the Pennines. Passenger services through the tunnel ran between Manchester and Sheffield, and these were withdrawn on 4 January 1970; freight survived until 1981. The track was then lifted east of Hadfield, where the present local passenger service terminates. A residual single track for freight remains over the last short section from Deepcar into Sheffield.
CW11323 - H. Cartwright

Above: English Electric locomotives no. E3027 (nearer the camera) and sister no. E3028 were built in 1960 for the 25kV ac from Manchester Piccadilly and what would become the West Coast main line electrification generally. They are here awaiting departure from Manchester Piccadilly on 22 August 1961 with the 16:00 to Crewe. Crewe was the extent of the initial system, to which would be added Liverpool Lime Street and then, progressively, sections to London Euston. These locomotives were also known as AL3s and would later become Class 83s. *B Wadey*

Opposite Top: The core part of Manchester Piccadilly, seen here on 14 February 1961, has a pleasant open-ness about it; this picture was taken from the overbridge which links the main platforms roughly half way along their length and leads to the side, through platforms, for trains to Oxford Road and beyond. The train in the nearby platform has destination boards claiming it is a Birmingham to Manchester service and also one from Manchester to Birmingham. Such boards were discarded by the 1970s, as they were considered too much of a safety risk for staff who had to reposition them between successive journeys. *AHR - Alan Roscoe*

Opposite Bottom: This 4-4-2T no. 67400 in 1908 was the first of the C13 class. Forty were to be built at Gorton workshops to a design by the Chief Mechanical Engineer, J G Robinson, of the Great Central Railway. It was seen at what was then Manchester London Road, later Piccadilly, looking very smart. Later rebuilt with superheater, the power classification was a modest Class 2 for passenger and Class 1 for freight. Eight of them, but not including this one, were fitted for push-pull operation. *NS202681 - Neville Stead*

Below: Time passes, but W A Stanier still thought it fit in 1932 to build a set of 10 Midland-style 0-4-4T locomotives with a 2P classification. No. 41908, seen here at Longsight depot between Manchester and Stockport on 5 July 1961, was one of these. They were provided with a push-pull capability. 41908 was withdrawn the following month and cut up. Somewhat unusually for a smallish tank engine, it had been given the British Railways mixed traffic livery, where the overall black was lined out in red and grey. *NS203559 - Neville Stead*

Opposite Top: Five types of electric locomotive (AL1 to AL5) were delivered from different manufacturers from about 1960 for the original West Coast electrification. These were followed from 1985 by a batch of 100 of a consolidated design built by both BR Doncaster and Vulcan Foundry. No. E3118 (later no. 86.041) is seen in the Manchester Piccadilly platforms. The train consisted of a Mk 2 non air-conditioned Brake First, followed by at least two Mk1 First vehicles. This became a standard arrangement, with First Class vehicles at the London end of the formation and Second (Standard) class at the other. *No record*

Opposite Bottom: With the overhead wires between Manchester Piccadilly and Crewe going live, local electric services were provided by the then new AM4 (later Class 304) four coach units. This formation formed of one unit no. 021 is seen heading for the side platforms nos 13 and 14. The rear blind offered only Manchester, so whether or not it would continue to Oxford Road was not stated. The date is 14 June 1961. *AHR - Alan Roscoe*

Opposite Top: Electrically hauled passenger services started to run between Manchester Piccadilly and Crewe on 12 September 1960. Here, AL1 (later Class 81) no. E3001 is seen in Longsight depot on 9 March of that year. It appears to have arrived from the manufacturers Associated Electrical Industries (AEI), been taken straight out of the box, and put on one side for somebody to decide what to do with it next. *No record*

Opposite Bottom: Hughes/Fowler 5MT 2-6-0 no. 42858 passes Heaton Norris, a short distance north of Stockport Edgeley, with a passenger service. The box is delicately located in between the up and down fast lines, so signalmen needed to take extra care when entering or leaving. A selection of goods vehicles can be seen here on both sides of the running lines. This is also the junction for Guide Bridge and Stalybridge, over which there is a one train a week from Stockport, in one direction only, in operation. These are known as Parliamentaries; the service can only be withdrawn with Parliament's (in effect the Minister's) approval, but it is can be easier and less consuming of management time to keep running a minimal service than to go through the vast rigmarole of service withdrawal. The key here is that the track is used for other than local passenger services anyway. *NS203836 - Neville Stead*

Above: This is the view northwards towards Manchester from Stockport Edgeley platforms. On the right is one of the longest surviving, old style and decidedly large, signal boxes, Stockport Edgeley No 2. Size is a benefit in that it allows signalling staff to keep an eye on what is going on over a larger area and plan accordingly; on the other hand, and depending on the number of signalmen on duty, they can cover considerable distances during a shift. That takes time as well as effort. Beyond the box can be seen this end of the 597 yards of Stockport Viaduct. The 27 spans include those over the River Mersey. On it, what is perhaps a Class 25 with a single parcels van can be seen on the down slow line, with a diesel unit in the far distance. *PY101465 - Henry Priestley*

Above: In the down side bay at Stockport Edgeley on 5 July 1961, this 5MT 2-6-0 was a joint Hughes/Fowler design and no. 42701 is arriving with a passenger service. These locomotives were easily distinguished by the great size of their cylinders and the substantial step up needed by the staff to get along the full length of the running plate. A total of 245 were built. *AS K64-4 - Alec Swain*

Opposite Top: The Royal Scot 4-6-0s of 1927 were created under the direction of Sir Henry Fowler, Chief Mechanical Engineer of LMS from 1925 to 1931. The 71 tender locomotives were rebuilt by his successor, Sir William Stanier, from 1935 onwards. Rebuilding included redesigned cylinders and valves, double blast pipe and chimney, but what really altered their appearance was the addition of redesigned smoke deflectors which curved around the boiler. No. 46111 *Royal Fusilier* is seen at the London end of the up main line platform at Stockport Edgeley in April 1960. The availability of a water crane here to replenish supplies will be noted. *NS203837 - Neville Stead*

Opposite Bottom: *The Comet* was a Restaurant Car Express from London to Manchester. This is the returning up train on 5 July 1961 calling at Stockport Edgeley (at 18:07) to pick up passengers only. The locomotive is no. D228, an English Electric Type 4 2,000hp diesel (later Class 40), but rather underpowered at that. These had to suffice until electrification in 1966/67. The leading vehicle is a British Railways CK (Corridor Compartment) fitted with Commonwealth bogies. These were a stop gap measure to meet justified complaints of the poor riding quality of the BR Mark 1 coaches. *AS K64-2 - Alec Swain*

Above: In this undated picture, Stockport Edgeley shed 9B sees LMS Class 8F 2-8-0 no. 48345, together with BR Class 9F 2-10-0 no. 92160. The latter has a chalked on number where its smokebox plate used to be. Neither are in tip top condition, but the second 9F in the distance is so filthy that it cannot be identified. Sadly, in the closing years of steam traction, locomotive cleaning was not a priority. Did the maintenance receive proper attention? *PY102265 - Henry Priestley*

Opposite Top: Macclesfield Hibel Road sees no. 42609, a Stanier 2-cylinder 2-6-4T from 1935. It was based at Stockport Edgeley shed, 9B, and will have brought in a train from Manchester via Guide Bridge and Rose Hill, Marple. It is seen here taking water in the course of running round its train. Rationalisation under British Railways was certainly necessary and this saw all traffic concentrated at the present Macclesfield station from 7 November 1960. Hibel Road was closed permanently. *4728 - Photographer Unknown*

Opposite Bottom: In October 1965, Macclesfield's only present station sees a Derby Lightweight 2-car DMU arriving on the route from Manchester via Rose Hill, Marple. This line was closed south of Rose Hill on 5 January 1970, and its track bed now forms part of the Middlewood Way, for walkers and other recreational users. The signal box carries the dated description of Macclesfield Old, though the previous station, more or less on this site, was named Macclesfield Central. History with matters railway never quite seems to go away. *PY10020N8 - Henry Priestley*

Opposite Top: An AM10 unit, later Class 310 no. 072 arrives at Macclesfield from Crewe, with a train for Manchester Piccadilly. It is 21 June 1969. These units, dating from 1965 and the very similar Class 312s from a decade later, were the last electric suburban units to be built with slam rather than sliding doors for passengers. Slam doors cannot shut themselves, and good punctuality depends on passengers shutting them after joining or alighting. Otherwise, you need platform staff, but they aren't going to spend all their time running up and down platforms to get trains away, and Guards are not going to be too keen, either. *PY1002N8 - Henry Priestley*

Opposite Bottom: AM4 electric unit no. 304.045 has left Goostrey with a up line service from Manchester Piccadilly to Crewe. These trains, with their slam doors, were close copies of those built for similar types of operation in North East London. In neither case did they distinguish themselves. A member of the platform staff is returning to the down platform by means of the barrow crossing. A down train is clearly expected here shortly. The shelter visible on the other platform demonstrates the new look then being provided for station development. It is 21 July 1962. *PY10074G - Henry Priestley*

Below: Crewe station sees Ivatt 2-6-2T no. 41225 with the16:32 push and pull train to Northwich. This service, by then only four trains per day over the branch via Middlewich was withdrawn on 4 January 1960. The branch itself is still extant, for freight, but also as a diversionary route. On the left is a BRC&W dmu (later Class 104), which will form the 16:57 to Manchester Piccadilly via Altrincham. Some interesting rail event seems to be expected, judging by the number of people on the footbridge. Or was it usually like this? Crewe, from anybody's point of view, is a busy station, for people changing trains (there is quite a choice of destinations) or merely as a start or end point to their journeys. *WS491 - W. A. C. Smith*

Manchester, South Junction & Altrincham

Opposite Top: Class 3MT 2-6-2T was a Fowler production of 1930; the outside steam pipes were a later addition. No. 40001 is seen here at Manchester Piccadilly on a local service, in a platform then used also by Manchester South Junction and Altrincham (MSJ&A) trains, as the overhead electrification indicates. This is at 1,500v dc, later to be converted to 25kV ac to allow through running by ac trains to Altrincham. Later still, with the coming of Manchester Metrolink, British Rail trains were rerouted from Piccadilly to reach Altrincham (and stations beyond) via Stockport. This added considerably to journey times. *NS203831 - Neville Stead*

Opposite Bottom: If the MSJ&A trains from Altrincham were to terminate at Oxford Road instead of Piccadilly, new platforms would need to be built in order to accommodate them. Such work on the north side of the station was seen under way here on 12 May 1956.The platforms also needed to be long enough to fully accommodate six car trains, each formed of two 185ft sets. This was incorporated in the general station remodelling, that included station buildings which would later win design awards. *AEB119OC - A.E Bennett*

Below: Oxford Road station is seen here on 22 July 1969, with one new platform in use and the second one at an advanced stage of construction. In Platform 5 may be seen an MSJ&A electric set, with Driving Trailer no. M29243M leading. Though only 58ft 1in long, these seated six-a-side in each of nine compartments. Such vehicles could therefore accommodate 108 seated passengers (6x2x9). That's not bad going where space is at a premium. There would however be fewer seats in the other vehicles of the set, making allowance for the Guard and general van space for prams, parcels etc. Overall, 24 First Class and 240 Second Class seats were provided in a three car set. *AS Y23-2 - Alec Swain*

Opposite Top: Steaming through Manchester Oxford Road on 3 May 1960 is Jubilee 4-6-0, no. 45599 *Bechuanaland*. These were Stanier locomotives of power class 6P5F and were a development of the Patriots. This large class of 191 locomotives was delivered between 1934 and 1936. Later modifications within the class included some fitted with a selection from roller bearings, Caprotti valve gear and double chimneys. This continued into British Railways days. A more recent difficulty with this section of line has been congestion caused by the new Ordsall Chord. This offers a direct rail route between Manchester Victoria, Deansgate and Oxford Road. It appealed to the politicians, but not the professionals. It does not link the two parts of the system adequately due to lack of capacity and the time taken to negotiate it, but neither does it help with the considerable problem of the in-town distribution of those arriving by train at either Victoria or Piccadilly. Those problem remains unresolved. *AS H59-1 - Alec Swain*

Opposite Bottom: What looks like a spanking new diesel unit is seen standing at Oxford Road on 3 May 1960. M 51423 was a Derby Lightweight Driving Motor Brake Second, coupled to a Driving Motor Composite with Lavatory. Although diesel units of this vintage have all been withdrawn (they would by now be around 60 years old), the comparison with what was by then ancient steam hauled compartment stock was very much to their credit. The shortcoming of the early diesel units generally was multiple designs from many different manufacturers, with those from one not necessarily compatible with those from the others. *AS H69-2 - Alec Swain*

Above: Ivatt 2-6-2T no. 41283 was one of a tapered boiler design of 1946. In the years that followed, 130 examples of this well received locomotive were built, to be followed by a very similar BR Standard build. The train is seen leaving Brooklands MSJ&A station, probably on a service between Manchester Central and Chester Northgate. This is a push-pull working, seen here in the pushing mode. The ability to merely reverse the train at termini and not take time for 'running round' as with ordinary locomotives and hauled coaches was a real operational economy. *20387 - Photographer Unknown*

Opposite Top: One of the original 1931 MSJ&A electric units is seen starting away from Navigation Road station for Altrincham, over the level crossing. For many years, this was the only line in the area with overhead electrification and a note on clearances may be of interest. How much might these vary depending on location? The 1952 Working Instructions provided the information. It stated that 'The normal height of the contact wire is 16ft above rail level, but this could be reduced to 13ft 9in at overbridges and increased to 18ft at public level crossings (as here) and to 20ft in certain sidings and at specified water columns (for steam traction).' This did refer to 1,500v dc systems only. *AS Y22-1 - Alec Swain*

Opposite Bottom: By the date of this photograph, 22 July 1968, this MSJ&A electric set, headed by Driving Motor Brake no. M28581 (the M suffix seems to have been mislaid by now) was in British Rail blue livery with a full yellow front end. It is arriving at Altrincham's Platform 1. The vehicle in the centre is a Composite, with the First Class section denoted by the yellow line above the windows. The 1931 electrification at 1,500v dc and overhead current collection was a recommendation of the Weir Committee to the Minister of Transport in its 1927 report on the future standards to be adopted. Apart from the Altrincham line, and Manchester-Sheffield-Wath, the only other place dc overhead would appear (temporarily as it turned out) was Liverpool Street to Shenfield and later to Chelmsford/Southend. *AS Y20-4 - Alec Swain*

047 The electric rolling stock for the MSJ&A's 8.7 mile route was built by Metropolitan Carriage & Wagon and the three car sets had 40 First class and 228 Third class seats. Here, Driving Motor Brake no. M28571M in green livery is arriving at Altrincham, Platform 1. Each motor coach housed four 328hp motors, to provide an acceleration rate of 1.35mph per second and a maximum speed of 62.5mph. It was said, rather unkindly, that the motion of these trains in action was reminiscent of the initials of the original company: Many. Short. Jerks… and Awaaaayyyy. *AS Y21-5 - Alec Swain*

M.S.J.& A.R!
ANY PERSON EXCEPT
SERVANTS OF THE COMPANY
'ON DUTY' CROSSING OR
WALKING ALONG THE LINE
WILL BE PROSECUTED

Opposite: An unusual bracket signal with a calling on arm could be found at Altrincham's Platform 2. The calling on facility is to permit a second train, which has already been halted, to then proceed at a slow and controlled pace towards a stationary one in front, usually to enable the two to be coupled up. That way, such manoeuvres can be carried out safely and efficiently. However, upper quadrant semaphore signals near overhead wires are not a good idea, hence the special arrangement seen here. *AS Y20-5 - Alec Swain*

Above: This trespass notice seen at Altrincham in 1968 stated that persons crossing the line or walking along it would be prosecuted. To make it completely clear, it further emphasised that this included servants of the company, *unless they were doing so in the course of their duty*. So servants were actually expected to comply with the by-laws and be faced with the legal enforcement if they did not. This then led to the problem of who is going to be around to carry out the enforcement? *AS Y21-3 - Alec Swain*

Opposite Top: Manchester Central station dated from 1880 and the general design of the train shed was very similar to that of St Pancras, built in 1868. The overall roof at 210 ft wide was narrower than the 245 ft of the London station, though it was very impressive all the same. Where there was a decided difference was the incorporation of a hotel beyond the buffer stops in London as part of the station frontage, but in Manchester the Midland Hotel was built on a nearby but wholly separate site. In this 1964 view, a Stanier Class 5 no. 45150 of Macclesfield depot stands, tender first, in Platform 5, on what is presumed to be an empty stock working. *MC10044M - A.W. V. Mace*

Opposite Bottom: A post-grouping development of the Midland Railway's Compound, these Johnson 4-4-0s were introduced in 1924. No. 41185 is at the head of the 12:25 express service from Manchester Central, seen here in Platform 5, to Nottingham. It is 3 September 1957. In Britain, the Compound locomotive, so called because it had both high and low pressure cylinders, was originated by S W Johnson of the Midland in 1902. The concept was improved by his successor Deeley, and then again by Fowler. Together, 45 such locomotives were built between 1902 and 1909. They were to be followed by a further 195 locomotives built under London, Midland & Scottish Railway auspices from 1924 to 1932. No 41185 was from the latter batch, being from the Vulcan Foundry build of 1927; it survived in traffic until 1957. The last Compounds were withdrawn from service in 1961. *WS628 - W. A. C Smith*

Above: Manchester Central sees no. 42598, a Stanier 2-cylinder design dating from 1935. The last passengers are hurrying to board this local train from Platform 4. On the right is no. 69801 in the engine release roads between Platforms 5 and 6. This is a Class A5 4-6-2T Robinson design of 1911 for the Great Central. In the foreground is a holder for the series of destination displays which might be needed from time to time. *NS203834 - Neville Stead*

Opposite Top: The turntable holds Fairburn no. 42137, a 4MT 2-6-4T development of Stanier's design and introduced in 1946. It is 3 May 1960. The London, Midland and Scottish company constructed well over 600 2-6-4Ts of this general type and they were to be found all over its system. Their main usage was for local passenger services. These and similar locomotives were around 48ft long and weighed in the region of 90 tons. Whatever might be used to turn them had to be correspondingly robust. Fortunately, tank engines were designed to be driven either smokebox or bunker first; this did help and was a characteristic much in their favour. *AS H68-4 - Alec Swain*

Opposite Bottom: In the not very attractive setting of Heaton Mersey shed may be seen no. 69331. This was a 3MT 0-6-2T design of 1891 by T Parker, Chief Mechanical Engineer of the Manchester, Sheffield & Lincolnshire Railway, 1886-93. It was classified as an N5 and this particular locomotive was withdrawn in 1957. At its maximum, there were around 120 locomotives of this general type. Whether or not this one retained until then the early written BRITISH RAILWAYS on the side tanks, as used before the advent of the 'cycling lion' emblem, is unknown. *REV97A-2-2 - Roy Vincent*

Above: The last of the British Railways Standard Classes to appear were the 9F 2-10-0s, which by British standards were truly massive machines. They were designed at Brighton, the first appearing in 1954 and the last, no 92250 *Evening Star*, in 1960. By all accounts they were very successful machines, and it was a pity that they came to the scene so late in the day. This is no. 92162 on the turntable at New Mills, with a number of vans in the background. Quite what was the function of the ladder seen here on the table is unclear, but who knew when someone might need to reach up high? It is 14 June 1961. *AHR - Alan Roscoe*

This is Chinley, where the 16:00 Derby to Manchester Central train is seen arriving on 21 April 1960 behind one of the short lived Metropolitan Vickers Co-Bo (or were they Bo-Co?) 1,200hp diesels, no. D5719. The train would have travelled by the direct route from Derby via Millers Dale to Chinley, which was closed north of Matlock on 6 March 1967. The alternative was (and is) to run via Chesterfield and the Hope Valley, tantalising close to but not reaching Sheffield. To do that, the locomotive would have had to run round its train at Sheffield to reverse directions, as well as covering a distance of an extra nine miles. Would the train paths and platform capacity be available? Could any line occupation problems be resolved? Could it be fitted into the train crew and rolling stock diagrams? What sort of obligations might the railway have in the services it provides? Who would lose out from journeys taking longer, and who would gain from the new opportunities it might offer? In short, would the time, cost and effort involved be worthwhile for either the railway or its passengers? These sorts of problems often confront the train planners. *AS H50-4 - Alec Swain*

Cheshire Lines

The Cheshire Lines Committee (CLC) was formed in 1863 and its 143 miles of route served Manchester, Chester, Warrington and Liverpool. This was a reaction to the monopolistic approach of the London & North Western Railway. CLC constituents were the Great Central, the Great Northern and, in 1866 the Midland, railway companies. Thus it included what would become Manchester Central station, of 1880. This picture shows the frontage of the Cheshire Lines goods warehouse in Winwick Street, Warrington as it was on 10 April 1960. Built in 1897, it is now a Grade II listed building. *AS H46-4 - Alec Swain*

Overleaf: The MSJ&A had its share of freight, some of which reached it via Deansgate Junction, seen here. This is where traffic from the Cheshire Lines Committee (CLC) railway joins it from the Stockport direction. The nearer overbridge carried the closed CLC route to Warrington, the further one what little is left of the former route towards Partington. This used to be a conventional double junction as seen here, but it has now been replaced by a pair of separate single track sections. Here, Stanier 8F 2-8-0 no. 48555 eases its load over the junction, which is a little north of Navigation Road station. *20540 - Photographer Unknown*

Opposite Top: Stanier 8F 2-8-0 no. 48511 gets its train on the way again on the MSJ&A towards Altrincham, a mere mile distant, after slowing for the Deansgate Junction intersection. Over this section to beyond Navigation Road station (about 30 chains). there are two parallel single lines, one each for National Rail and for Metrolink services. Two sets of parallel double lines then commence, though there is however a crossover between them. This is not used for passenger services, only for movements connected with infrastructure maintenance, for instance. *23479 - Photographer Unknown*

Opposite Bottom: The Ivatt 2-6-0 no. 43033 was a post war LMS design, the first examples of which just managed to appear before railway nationalisation in 1948. They were notable for their extremely high running plates, a feature which was to be repeated in the Ivatt tank locomotives and their successors generally. These included the BR Standard Class 4 (the 76000 class) and the whole range of Standard types. No. 43033 was delivered in 1949. It is seen at Deansgate Junction on a passenger service which was likely to have originated at Manchester Central. The locomotive was based at Trafford Park, 9E. *23481 - Photographer Unknown*

Above: Freight latterly became diesel hauled and Class 25 no. D7554 (later no 25.204) was photographed on 22 July 1968 heading through Platform 3 on the up line at Altrincham, towards Manchester. This and Platform 4 were (and still are) used also for the passenger services continuing towards Chester. The two platforms on the far side, nos 1 and 2, were used exclusively by the terminating electric passenger services, again these are now Manchester Metrolink services. *AS Y21-1 - Alec Swain*

Opposite Top: No. 42078 was a 1945 development by C E Fairburn of the Stanier designed 4MT 2-6-4T of 1933. It is seen here arriving at West Timperley with a local train en route from Warrington Central to Stockport Tiviot Dale. Local rail services and with them West Timperley station closed on 30 November 1964. Longer distance passenger services continued for another couple of years only, but goods services were brought to an end by the closure in 1984 of the bridge over the Manchester Ship Canal at Cadishead. That bridge required extensive repairs, which were considered unaffordable. As a result, a single track from Skelton Junction remains only as far as Partington. *23493 - Photographer Unknown*

Opposite Bottom: Class O4 2-8-0 no. 63794 was a rebuild of Robinson's 2-8-0 design of 1911; it is seen here passing Glazebrook, a Cheshire Lines Committee station, on 22 April 1960. The train is heading east towards Manchester and what is now the very congested section of track through Oxford Road station. But then of course it might have been taking the alternative route via Skelton Junction towards Stockport. Photographers rarely have the ability to enquire of the train crew (or others) where goods services are going. *AS H53-5 - Alec Swain*

Above: In original green livery with yellow lining and a 'v' warning on the cab front, these diesel units later became Class 108. They were built by Derby Workshops and this one is approaching from the Liverpool direction on the Cheshire Lines route. This is, or rather was, Glazebrook West Junction. The former Great Central line to Wigan Central and St Helens Central curves away to the right; the station itself is behind the photographer. Of the junction itself and the tracks leading from it, there is now no trace. *4660 - Photographer Unknown*

Opposite Top: An elderly Great Central class J10 3F 0-6-0 no. 65189 of 1901 vintage, by J G Robinson, was photographed at St Helens Central. Presumably it was in the course of running round its train. This would have come from Lowton St Mary's, 6¼ miles away, and itself on another branch line, 14 miles long, from Glazebrook to Wigan Central. Closure came to St Helens Central, which was a Great Central station, on 3 March 1952. The following British Railways press statement gives the background. 'During 1952, the policy was continued of closing branch lines where the volume of traffic did not justify their operation and could not be made to do so – in other words where there was little public demand. Forty branches, with a route mileage of 304, were authorised during the year for complete or partial closing. Eighty four stations were also closed'. This was during a time of serious national coal shortages. It might also be added that it was still 11 years before the publication of Dr Beeching's Reshaping Report, in 1963. *No record*

Opposite Bottom: Wigan Central station serving the line from Glazebrook sees a large LMS designed 2-6-4T placing a parcels van on the end of a passenger train in the station platform on 19 January 1960. It is not now easy to imagine a situation where such manoeuvres took place regularly, that there was locomotive power available to make such moves, that the track layouts allowed it to happen and that turnround times were sufficiently generous that there was time to do it. It just doesn't fit in with the reality of the diesel multiple unit. This line was opened on 13 October 1892 and closed to passengers on 2 November 1964; goods services followed on 5 April 1965. *PY1013WB - Henry Priestley*

Cheshire Lines

Opposite: The CLC line served Warrington Bank Quay Low Level station, seen here on 1 December 1959, with the back of a dmu from Manchester Oxford Road. This was bound for Ditton Junction, on the line from Crewe to Liverpool Lime Street. The pared down service to these platforms was withdrawn on 10 September 1962, although very occasional use was made of them for another three years until 1965. If passengers wanted to change between Warrington low and high level platforms, such an arrangement was considerably better than having to hike across town to Warrington Central, but it did of course depend on where they wanted to go. *AS G60-6 - Alec Swain*

Below: The delightfully named Slutchers Lane signal box, some distance to the east of Warrington Bank Quay Low Level station platforms. originally controlled the level crossing there. That was replaced by a road bridge and the box was moved to a location rather nearer the platform ends. It is seen here as it was on 10 April 1960. In 1953, *British Railways Facts and Figures* recorded that there were then 10,300 signal boxes on the system, the large majority being of this type. Today, such traditional signal boxes, large or small, are becoming a decided rarity. *AS H46-2 - Alec Swain*

Overleaf: The London, Midland & Scottish Railway had Sir William Stanier to thank for their fine Coronation Pacific locomotives. Here no. 46252 *City of Leicester* is seen near Warrington Bank Quay with a train of around ten coaches. These were a development of the earlier Princess class and were introduced in 1938. Twelve of the class of, eventually, 38 locomotives were streamlined as built, though no. 46252 was not one of them. Curiously, streamlining lasted through World War II, but was removed soon afterwards on the grounds of making maintenance easier. *NS203851 - Neville Stead*

Above: The main part of Warrington Bank Quay station sees an unidentified Ivatt 2-6-2T and its train, together with several trolleys used for parcels traffic. Handling parcels in quantity takes up time, both in terms of occupying staff and usage of the platform. Meanwhile, the train, which also has to have sufficient capacity. isn't moving and earning revenue. On the other hand, parcels traffic could be very profitable, especially in terms of newspaper and Post Office traffic, though the former has long deserted rail. Some limited Royal Mail movements may still be seen. *MC10006W - A. W. V. Mace*

Below: The Trans-Pennine units were built to provide a rather higher quality of service than was in place. Six-car sets of these new units were to offer what in 1961 approached a regular hourly service between Liverpool, Manchester, Huddersfield, Leeds and Hull. A welcome novelty was a Griddle Car, with bar. Here a set, later Class 124, is seen leaving Liverpool Lime Street in a cloud of exhaust fumes, led by Driving Motor Composite no. E51955. 'Speed, reliability and comfort' were the selling points, but it seems that these were not enough to counter the appeal of the M62, opened in stages from 1971 to 1976. The buffet cars were removed, and after a few years the whole concept faded gradually. Recent times have given some hope of its revival. *CM - Colin Martin*

The Class 6P5F 4-6-2 Standard locomotives, 'The Clans' were a slightly reduced version of the Britannia Class 7MT locomotives and spent most of their time in or around Scotland. Seen here, no. 72000 *Clan Buchanan* heads a train from Manchester Victoria which is passing through Manchester Exchange on its way north. Only 10 of these machines were built out of an originally intended total of 25; the unbuilt ones even had their names allocated! British Railways went as far as designing and building 12 different types of Standard steam locomotives, which between them were expected to meet future motive power needs. In the end, 999 such locomotive were actually built, the first appearing in 1951 and the last being withdrawn in 1968.
NS203832 - Neville Stead

Above: Between Manchester Exchange's Platform 4 (left) and Platform 3 (right) was the line known as the Down Through, and this was used by trains starting from Manchester Victoria but passing through Manchester Exchange without stopping. Standard Class 5 4-6-0 no. 73157 is heading one such train. On the right passengers are leaving a train which has terminated in Platform 2. The station ceased to be used by passenger services on 5 May 1969, though its newspaper traffic continued for at least a further decade. *LT(2) - Leslie Turner*

Below: No. 49199 was a later rebuild of one of the London & North Western Railway G1 class with a Belpaire firebox. It was introduced by Bowen-Cooke and dated from 1912. These were powerful 0-8-0s with a 7F rating after their rebuilding. It is on the Down Through line, a little on the west side of Manchester Exchange station. These were sizeable premises, though their utility was not perhaps as high as it might have been. *NS203822 - Neville Stead*

The Northern Dales Rail Tour, seen here at Manchester Victoria on 4 September 1955, was a joint enterprise between the Stephenson and the Manchester locomotive societies. It was to travel via Blackburn and Hellifield to Tebay, where engines were changed. The locomotive seen here was no. 41102, a post-Grouping 1924 development of the Midland Compound 4-4-0, then allocated to Blackpool shed, 24E. The fireman standing on the tender is bringing the coal forward, to make his life easier subsequently when shovelling it into the firebox. The only overhead electric railway power lines then in the area were on the MSJ&A. *AEB 8588 - A. E Bennett*

Page 55 Top: No. 42180 was the post-war development of the 1927 design of 2-6-4Ts by Fowler for the London Midland & Scottish company. The train is leaving Manchester Victoria's no 12 Platform with corridor stock, so presumably this was on a longer distance journey. From the passengers' point of view, the provision of toilets on such trains could make them rather more attractive than non-corridor trains, with 'straight through' compartments only. They also gave one more control over in whose company you sat. On train ticket issue and/or inspection were both more achievable. *NS203821 - Neville Stead*

Page 55 Bottom: This clean and probably recently delivered Cravens diesel unit is seen at Platform 12 at Manchester Victoria on 7 October 1959. It would appear to be in the course of leaving in a westerly direction, but the destination blind still shows Manchester. Perhaps the train crew haven't got used to such technological advances yet? These trains were designed for, relatively speaking, rural operations, but it may be noted that, unusually, the unit consists of a pair of power cars instead of one power and one trailer. There are, after all, quite a few stiff gradients to be encountered around Manchester. Only two slam doors were provided for passengers on each side of each vehicle. That is fine for fitting in more seating, but it will not allow speedy passenger entrance and exit at busy stations. The classic mismatch was when a number of similar units (one power, one trailer) were allocated to King's Cross inner suburban operations; they stayed there for years. Their later classification was as Class 105; all were gone by 1989. *ASG21-3 - Alec Swain*

Above: This Britannia hauled rail tour is seen here at Manchester Victoria, prior to its departure in a westerly direction at 10.00 on 19 March 1967. The newly painted locomotive is no. 70015 *Apollo*, distinguishable as one of those built new for the Western Region, with grab holes in the smoke deflectors for the crew, rather than hand rails. The train is *The Lancastrian Rail Tour* for the Railway Correspondence and Travel Society and would be visiting Bury, Todmorden, Blackburn, Bolton, Southport and Eccles, before arriving at Manchester Piccadilly at 17.54, 167 miles and 9 chains later. The direct distance, start to finish, is about one mile – but you had to walk it, take a bus or a taxi. *NS203830 - Neville Stead*

Patricroft shed (26F) sees one of Bowen-Cooke's G1 0-8-0 locomotives, no. 48926, plus part of another. They were introduced in 1912 but rebuilt from 1936 with a G2a boiler and Belpaire firebox. This uplifted their power rating from 6F to 7F capability. The G1, G2 and G2A classes together amounted to 502 locomotives. They were versatile in the uses to which they could be put, but for a time became what amounted to the standard heavy freight locomotive of the LMS. The last two of these were still on the books right through to 1964. Their position was only challenged by Sir William Stanier's 8F class, which first saw the light of day in 1935. The 8Fs ran to an eventual 666 locomotives in British Railways service, excluding those which never returned from overseas duties during WW11. These two G1 derivatives were photographed on 31 August 1958. They were unusual in not having smokebox number plates. *ASE8-2 - Alec Swain*

Opposite: Seen here on 21st August 1964 is no. 42961, a 5MT locomotive of the 2-6-0 wheel arrangement, also known as a Mogul. The origin of that name is obscure, but it seems to derive from American sources and refers to the importance of having the two leading wheels to guide the six driving wheels. These locomotives were designed at Horwich under the direction of Sir William Stanier, but built at Crewe. The class extended to 40 locomotives, which were introduced in 1933 and all survived until the mass withdrawals from 1963 onwards. The scene is Hindley North, where no. 42961 is hauling a train of vans, which will proceed eastbound via Bolton. *FM53-2 - Larry Fullwood*

Above: In 1963, Wigan shed sees no. 42554, a Stanier 2-cylinder 2-6-4T of 1935. This was a popular wheel arrangement for locomotives designed to haul fast moving outer-suburban trains and there were many examples of similar types for services around the big cities. You couldn't really call no. 42554 clean, but it does perhaps display a consistent light grey finish all over. In the background is no. 44240, a post grouping 1924 development of the Midland 0-6-0 4F design and of which 580 examples were built. *NS203839 - Neville Stead*

Above: 4F no. 44222 has been decidedly spruced up at Wigan shed. Was it for some special occasion perhaps, or was it always kept like that? It carries a 27D Wigan L&Y shed plate, so it could usually be found here when not at work. Wigan shed closed in 1964 and no. 44222 was withdrawn from service with it, presumably no longer required either. *NS203526 - Neville Stead*

Opposite Top: This 1949 photograph show no. 52727, a survivor from the Lancashire & Yorkshire Railway's Class 30 and seen here at Wigan shed. These were 0-8-0s, rated as 6Fs and built by J F Aspinall. Three members only of the original build of 60 locomotives made it past 1 January 1948 and thus into very early British Railways days. Built in 1903, this locomotive was one of them; it is recorded as having been withdrawn on 14 October 1950. The eight wheeled tender may be noted. *NS204055 - Neville Stead*

Opposite Bottom: In what amounts to an almost head on view, Aspinall Lancashire & Yorkshire Class 27 0-6-0 no. 52197, with 3F capability, is seen from a passenger train which it is passing. Built in May 1893, withdrawal came on 15 May 1956. Its shed code of 27D refers to it being based at Wigan, Lancashire & Yorkshire, to distinguish it from the 8F code of Springs Branch (Wigan), the North Western shed. *CW11496 - H. Cartwright*

Above: The tracks at Wigan Wallgate pass below the road of that name on which the main station buildings and ticket office stand. Reaching the rather dismal platform area meant descending to the lower level by a long slope. Here, puddles remain on the platform, probably from leaks in the roof, but it was a generally murky day. Lancashire & Yorkshire stations tended to be places where you would not spend more time than absolutely necessary, and this one was no exception. The track on the far right has since been lifted. *MC10025N - A. W. V Mace*

Opposite Top: This is the Springs Branch shed at Wigan in 1955 with no. 52341, an Aspinall L&Y 0-6-0. For all steam locomotives, irrespective of origin or shed, this was a fruitful source of coal and water. No. 52341 was one of 484 similar machines of L&YR Class 27, built between 1889 and 1918. They were designed by Aspinall and built at the company's Horwich workshops. Haulage of goods services was their primary occupation. All had been withdrawn by 1962 but 63 were rebuilt to Class 28. This meant that the firebox was replaced by one of Belpaire design and larger cylinders were fitted. These were all scrapped by 1957. Also to be seen is part of Stanier 2-6-4T no. 42465. *NS203952 - Neville Stead*

Opposite Bottom: An interloper reached Wigan in 1954 but maybe it had more substantial business there than that of a mere visitor. This is no. 65199, a Robinson J10 class 2F 0-6-0 of 1901. These were built for the Great Central Railway, originally as 9Ds or 9Hs. Including variations, a total of 124 were built, of which 78 survived to be passed to British Railways. No. 65199 has stopped close to the water tank, but not quite close enough to imbibe. Or perhaps the driver considered it had no need? Eight of these J10s were moved to the London & North Western's shed of Springs Branch in 1952, where it seems that they were well received and were used extensively on lines in the Wigan area. The last two J10s were withdrawn from this shed in 1961. *NS202634A - Neville Stead*

Opposite Top: Wigan North Western station entrance, although only a short distance from Wallgate station, is below the level of the railway. Few locations are at their best when it is raining as hard as in this picture, but it was not very enticing even in bright sunshine. It hardly conveys the exciting modern InterCity image, though such concepts were all but unheard of when this picture was taken, perhaps in about 1967. Presentation is not everything by any stretch of the imagination, but it does merit some consideration. It was certainly not something which was at the top the list in the first couple of decades of railway nationalisation, but then it was a continuing struggle to get it all working passably well and to keep it so. *MC14007W - A. W. V Mace*

Opposite Bottom: An Ivatt 2-6-2T no. 41211 is ready to take this push and pull formation away from Wigan North Western on a stopping passenger working in 1961. Its destination is not recorded, but similar make ups of train were then commonplace over the north west of Britain generally. By this time, diesel multiple units were becoming available in quantity, though how they were to be rationed out to the various Regions and then the lines within them was another matter. Careful evaluation, or heated discussion? The perilous financial situation of British Railways was by then becoming clear; what would happen under the new British Railways Board to be created on 1 January 1963 with its new Chairman, Dr Richard Beeching? *NS203853 - Neville Stead*

Below: In this 1961 picture, Jubilee 4-6-0 no. 45703 *Thunderer* is hurrying a mixed freight south through Wigan North Western. The lamps on the front of the locomotive signify that it is a Class 5 working, with not less than 50% of its train being fitted with continuous brakes. That is relevant in terms of the braking distance needed and hence its maximum permitted speed. This main line was frequented by quantities of express passenger and also goods traffic; it is also extremely busy today. *NS203854 - Neville Stead*

Opposite: No. 86.236 approaches Wigan North Western in September 1974 with two members of staff in the cab. What were, and were not, suitable staffing levels for various tasks was not a problem for the railway industry alone, but there were few ways forward on which management and trades unions seemed to be able to find agreement. The single manning of even freight trains then had some way to go, and the problem has yet to be fully solved for passenger operations. This train was 6P40, which would have been enough to tell all those with access to the Working Timetable what they needed to know about it, but head codes have long been replaced with non-communicating headlamps. *AWB - Arnold Battson*

Below: One of the production Class 86 locomotives for the Euston, Birmingham, Manchester and Liverpool electrification heads south with a cement train through Wigan North Western in May 1975. This is no. 86.232, later named *Harold Macmillan* after the Prime Minister from 1957 to 1963. It was he who on 10 March 1960 said 'First the industry must be of a size and pattern suited to modern conditions and prospects. In particular, the railway system must be remodelled to meet current needs, and the modernisation plan must be adapted to this new shape.' Such was the background to 'The Reshaping of British Railways', also known as the Beeching plan, published by the British Railways Board in March 1963. On a much lighter note, the picture also shows the Swan & Railway public house. This could be a welcome sight for arriving passengers, opposite as it is to the station exit. *AWB - Arnold Battson*

Above: The Railway Correspondence & Travel Society and the Stephenson Locomotive Society organised a massive trip, the *Aberdeen Flyer*. This started from London King's Cross at 08:00 on 2 June 1962 behind the London & North Eastern Railway's no. 60022 *Mallard* and returned from Aberdeen to Euston after a trip to Inverurie and back. LMS 4-6-2 no. 46200 *The Princess Royal* (12A Carlisle Kingmoor) headed the train south from Carlisle, stopping at Crewe to detach four sleeping cars and to add two Open Seconds and a 1924-built gas-lit Kitchen car. It then continued to London Euston. It is seen here taking water during a stop at Wigan North Western; Euston arrival at 14:23 on 3 June was roundly three hours late. According to the tickets, this was euphemistically deemed to be a 'Day Excursion'. *LRF7149 - Leslie R Freeman*

Opposite Top: The Crewe to Glasgow electrification of 1975 was accompanied by a new build of 35 Class 87 locomotives. These 25kV ac 100 mph machines were intended to give their trains extra 'oomph' as they tackled the banks of Shap and Beattock. In any event, more electric locomotives were required, and these replaced the Class 50 diesel electrics which, in pairs, had hauled such trains north of Crewe. The latter found new employment elsewhere, notably on the South Western main line between Waterloo and Exeter. No. 87.010 in British Rail blue, later named *King Arthur*, is seen at Wigan North Western on its way north. *AWB - Arnold Battson*

Opposite Bottom: A Fairburn designed 2-6-4T no. 42292 of 1945 vintage is seen arriving at Manchester Victoria from the east on 8 October 1959. When the London, Midland & Scottish Railway decided that they wanted large tank engines for their suburban or other traffic, they certainly went ahead and built them in quantity. No fewer than seven design variations appeared from three successive Chief Mechanical Engineers over the 1927-47 period, resulting in a total of 645 locomotives. Steam haulage of what mostly amounted to outer suburban passenger rail services confirms what a long time ago it was. *ASG22-5 - Alec Swain*

Designed at Derby, Henry Fowler's Royal Scot 4-6-0s of 1927 were a class which extended to 71 locomotives. They were rebuilt by Stanier from 1943 onwards with taper boilers, new cylinders and double chimneys. Here, unrebuilt no. 46137 *Prince of Wales Volunteers (South Lancashire)*, puts on a spirited performance as it takes its train through Manchester Victoria station before it reaches the bank of 1 in 59, steepening to 1 in 47, which will take it to Miles Platting. This was the last of the 'Scots' to be rebuilt, for which it had to wait until 1955. *NS202828 - Neville Stead*

Towards Bolton

Top: This is Fowler's 1929 design of 0-8-0 for the London Midland & Scottish Railway classified as a 7F. No. 49627 was seen at Agecroft shed on 26 August 1959. This and similar locomotives always seemed to have very flat fronted smokebox doors. *ASF62-2 - Alec Swain*

Bottom: On 26 August 1959 Lancs & Yorks 2F 0-6-0ST no. 51458 was an 1891 Aspinall rebuild of his predecessor Barton Wright's Class 23, which dated back to 1877. The main use of the rebuilds was shunting and trip working, and there were 230 of them. This rather depressing scene at Agecroft shed suggests that the time is all but up for this locomotive, but it was over 80 years old by then. In fact, it had already been withdrawn three months earlier, on 31 May 1959. *ASF63-3 - Alec Swain*

Above: A 'Black 5' or more correctly a Stanier 5MT 4-6-0 no. 45227, of a design first built in 1934, is in charge of the 15:20 Blackpool Central to Manchester Victoria. It is passing through Clifton Junction, a station with only a modest catchment area, on 5 July 1963. The class extended to no fewer than 842 locomotives; not many others were built in such quantities. The junction ceased to exist with the closure of the section of the line to Radcliffe (not in view). *FM42-5 - Larry Fullwood*

Opposite Top: Stanier 2-cylinder 2-6-4T no. 42444 of 1935 build is seen on a train from Manchester Victoria. It is taking what to it was the left hand (more westerly) route past Clifton Junction signal box towards Bolton and eventually its destination of Horwich. It is 5 July 1963. Horwich was on a short branch from Blackrod and latterly services were at times required by the works only. That branch closed on 27 September 1965. The easterly route led to Radcliffe and Bury; most of that closed on 5 December 1968 and the track was lifted. *FM42-4 - Larry Fullwood*

Opposite Bottom: A former War Department 2-8-0 no. 90207 passes through Clifton Junction from the Bolton line with a lengthy mixed freight train on 21 August 1964. An attempt has been made to paint a face on the smokebox door, with what success or otherwise the reader may judge. Freight tonnages by the type of goods carried (national figures) were coal 60%, minerals 22% and merchandise 18%. Coal traffic in those days was vital to the railway, as indeed the railway was vital to the prosperity of the mines. The station became plain Clifton in 1974. *FM52-2 - Larry Fullwood*

Opposite Top: Hughes 'Crab' 2-6-0 no. 42714 is seen in charge of an excursion to Blackpool on 19 August 1961, with a train made up of some of the most decrepit rolling stock around. It is passing Bolton Trinity Street station. In another 18 months, Dr Beeching was to make scathing comments about the number of passenger vehicles which saw only minimal use. His Reshaping Report stated that a large number of the coaches available for high peak traffic were only required on a limited number of occasions per year, namely 2,000 on not more than 10, another 2,000 on not more than 14 and a third 2,000 on not more than 18. The annual provision cost of this fleet was put at £3.4m, against which they earned only 0.5m. Something was going to have to change. *FM25-5 - Larry Fullwood*

Opposite Bottom: An up service for Manchester Victoria is seen at Bolton's one time Trinity Street station, with a 4-6-0 of the Patriot class no. 45550 in charge. This was a 6P7F locomotive from 1933 to Fowler's design and was one of the 10 in the class of 52 that was never named. The two centre tracks at Bolton station have now been removed, but what remains is now electrified. This includes the route to Euxton Junction and thus the West Coast main line, as well as towards Manchester. *NS203850 - Neville Stead*

Above: Lancashire & Yorkshire 2P 2-4-2T locomotive no. 50731, seen at Bolton, was from a group of locomotives rebuilt with a firebox which had a square shaped cross section. This was designed by the Belgian engineer Belpaire. Compared with the round top and until then usual version, it gives a greater surface area at the top, where the heat is greatest, thus enhancing heat transfer and steam production. The fitting of Belpaire-inspired fireboxes became a common modification to locomotive fleets generally. *PH000621 - Peter Hay*

Above: Immediately north of Bolton station and controlled by the Bolton West signal box, the line from Manchester divides. Trains for the Blackburn direction take the far line; others continue to the left and, on reaching Lostock Junction three miles further on, they then turn right for Preston or left for Wigan Wallgate. This mildly vertiginous footbridge gave excellent views of proceedings here. *PY102018 - Henry Priestley*

Opposite Top: Just north of Bolton Trinity Street station 1889 Aspinall Class 5 2-4-2T no. 50646 is seen, complete with a coach containing six compartments and the guard's brake for push pull operation. It is 14 April 1951. This locomotive is one of the earlier versions which were given a short bunker with limited coal capacity and it retained a round topped firebox. This extensive Lancashire & Yorkshire Railway class, with a large number of variations introduced over the years, were classified as 2P by British Railways. *PP665 - Peter Pescod*

Opposite Bottom: This is Bolton shed (26C) in 1953. No. 50731 has its chimney towards the camera (locomotive with short bunker) and no. 50887 (with more capacious long bunker) facing away. In the distance is a coaling tower, a common sight in the larger sheds during the post-war period. Using gravity to fill locomotive tenders or bunkers was a vast improvement in both time and effort on the use of shovels by the staff. *NS204009A - Neville Stead*

Above: This close up view at Bolton of no. 50887, which was given 3P status, shows how the design of these locomotives had developed as the years progressed. This is a Hughes locomotive introduced in 1925, built with Belpaire firebox and extended smokebox. The longer style bunker has been very well filled; perhaps the locomotive was to be rostered for a longer journey? *NS204025A - Neville Stead*

Below: Stanier 3-cylinder 4MT 2-6-4T no. 42485 is looking very business-like as it stands over the pits of Lostock Hall, its home shed (24D), on 22 March 1960. It will have been one of the key members of that shed's fleet. The LMS was a huge undertaking, which also included some of the more profitable parts of the railways of Britain. Part of a Stanier Class 5, no. 45201, can also be seen. *ASH23-2 - Alec Swain*

Above: Large numbers of locomotives with substantial pulling power were deemed necessary for use by the armed forces at the outbreak of World War II in 1939. These were built for the Ministry of Supply in several railway workshops to a design by R A Riddles. They were likened to an economy (or austerity) version of a Stanier 8F. Introduction was from 1943. At the end of the conflict, many found their way to the nationalised British Railways. Included in them was 2-8-0 no. 90470, seen here at Lostock Hall on 29 March 1960. The austerity regime extended also to some very similar 2-10-0s, of which British Railways received 25. *ASH33-2 - Alec Swain*

Below: This Lancashire & Yorkshire Railway Public Notice reads 'All persons are hereby warned not to trespass on the railway or on any station or other access lands or property of the Lancs & Yorks Railway Co. Every person seen trespassing after this warning will be prosecuted and will be liable under Section 38 of the Lancs & Yorks Railway Act 1884 to a penalty not exceeding forty shillings. By Order.' That'll teach them! *ASH23-5 - Alec Swain*

Bury Electrics

One of the earliest beneficiaries of electric traction was the Manchester to Bury service of the Lancashire & Yorkshire Railway. This was opened to traffic on 7 April 1916 as a development of the electrification from Bury to Holcombe Brook (closed 1952). It used 1,200v dc supplied by side collection from an outside third live rail, protected by wooden guarding. This aimed to prevent ice forming on the live rail and hence interrupting electrical pick up. The standard formation was a 5-car train, seating 389 passengers (72 1st class and 312 2nd), with motor cars leading, in the centre, and trailing, plus two trailers. Unusually, a driving compartment was provided at each end of each car, giving maximum formation flexibility. Seen here is one such train arriving at Manchester Victoria from Bury. *WS299 - W. A. C. Smith*

Above: Bury Bolton Street was the terminus until Bury Interchange was built by the Passenger Transport Executive. Here, 5MT 2-6-0 no. 42731 sits in Platform 2 on 9 September 1959; while one of the then new electric units is seen in the distance, having departed for Bury from Platform 4. The line curving round to the left is the former Lancashire & Yorkshire line to Rochdale, part of the former route from Bolton. All the trackage in this picture and that behind the photographer, is now part of the East Lancashire Light Railway, a heritage line. Bury Interchange serves at the terminus for Manchester Metrolink; there are now no connections in Bury with National Railways. *ASF83-2 - Alec Swain*

Below: In 1959, the London Midland Region had built no fewer than 26 2-car units as replacement stock for their Manchester Victoria to Bury Bolton Street service. Seen here is Driving Trailer Composite no. M77162; the second vehicle will be a Motor Open Brake Second. This is a southbound working. Given that the 9¾ miles between the termini were usually covered in about 23 mins, one train could comfortably make the round trip in under the hour. A 4-car train had 356 seats (32 1st class and 324 2nd, so a four trains per hour service would offer 1,424 seats in each direction. This would use a mere 16 of the units in the fleet. By 1980, only 18 units of what were by then Class 504 remained in service, which still allowed for maintenance spares. *OTA0211 - Online Transport Archive*

J F Aspinall was the creator of the Lancashire & Yorkshire Railway's standard 0-6-0s built between 1889 and 1917. They were classified as Class 27 by the company and a remarkable 484 locomotives were built over the period. Nationalisation saw 246 or just over half of them handed to British Railways, which rated them as having 3F capability. No. 52108 is seen as awaiting a call to bank goods trains (or others in need) up the steep climb east of Manchester Victoria to Miles Platting; the date is 28 August 1959. The locomotive was withdrawn on 24 October of that year. *ASF64-1 - Alec Swain*

Not to be outdone was the very similar no. 52165 from the same L&Y class. But this locomotive is facing in the other direction and hence displaying its other side - at the same place and ready for the same purpose. It will be noted that this position was very handy for the water crane, needed as it almost certainly would be. No. 52165 was built at Horwich in April 1892 and would be succumbing to its final withdrawal on 6 April 1957. *NS204045 - Neville Stead*

A less common occupier of the siding at Manchester Victoria used principally for banking engines was Ivatt 2MT 2-6-0 no. 46487. It was built at Darlington in 1951, but withdrawn in 1963, rather earlier than most of its contemporaries. Known as the 'Mickey Mouse' engines for some inscrutable reason, as many as 128 were to appear before the design was superseded by the very similar BR Standard class in the 78000 number series. These accounted for a further 65 locomotives. ASD58-3 - Alec Swain

Below: Robinson Class O4 2-8-0 no. 63605 is in ex-works condition as it hauls a freight (or perhaps a parcels service) passing east through Manchester Victoria on the Down Main on 28 August 1959. This was a Great Central Railway design dating from 1911. Platform 11 at Manchester Victoria, from which this photograph was taken, was a rewarding place from which to view the passing scene, as long as it was not occupied by a train. *ASF64-3 - Alec Swain*

Opposite Top: Class O4 no. 63605 gets a clear road, at least until the next stop signal, as it proceeds up the bank towards Miles Platting on 28 August 1959. It may or may not be requiring banking assistance up the gradient which varies from 1 in 47 to 1 in 59. This was not a good place for trains which have to make a standing start. *ASF64-4 - Alec Swain*

Opposite Bottom: At one time, the eastern end of Manchester Victoria showed a huge display of semaphores controlled from Manchester Victoria East Junction signal box. That might be fine in good clear weather, but if the clouds thicken and the rain starts, visibility can be poor. It is 1 December 1959. They would also need a fair amount of maintenance; even refiling the oil lamps on each signal and trimming the wicks required a lot of ladder work. As a newcomer to the area in 1968, the author was warned: "if you can see the Pennines, that means it is going to rain. If you can't see them, it is already raining". *ASG60-4 - Alec Swain*

Newton Heath depot, 26A, was sited neatly in between the Calder Valley main line to Rochdale and beyond and the southern end of the Oldham loop, where that diverged. On 9 September 1959, the allocation was around 180 locomotives, all steam, and this section shows some of what might have been found there on a visit. At any one time, of course, some will be out and earning their keep, and others will be visitors. Classified 2F, 0-6-0ST no. 51343 was an 1891 rebuild by Aspinall of a class introduced by Barton Wright of the Lancashire & Yorkshire in 1877, one of a number to be found here. *AS F82-5 - Alec Swain*

Above: No. 52230 is an Aspinall 3F 0-6-0, derived from the original design of 1889. One of a dozen similar locomotives then based at Newton Heath, it is seen at shed on 10 September 1959. By then their numbers were fast shrinking. This must have been a hot day, to judge by the open cab spectacle plate being used to keep the footplate area at a reasonable temperature for the locomotive crew. *ASF84-2 - Alec Swain*

Overleaf Top: The 6P Jubilee 4-6-0s of 1934 could be described as 'Improved Patriots', and were built in considerable numbers for a locomotive classified as 6P. The final tally was 190 machines. It is 9 September 1959 and no. 45679 *Armada* was one of eight then based at Newton Heath. It was looking very respectable and ready for its next turn of duty. Newton Heath at 26A was a principal shed; smaller sheds were 26B Agecroft, 26C Bolton, 26D Bury, 26E Bacup and 26F Lees. Newton Heath remains in use today as a Traction Maintenance Depot (TMD). *ASF82-6 - Alec Swain*

Overleaf Bottom: This was one of the well known 'Jinty' 0-6-0Ts, Johnson's design for the Midland and introduced in1899. Originally built in February 1900 and rebuilt with a Belpaire firebox and improved cab around 1919, no. 47212 was classified as a 3F and was pictured at Newton Heath shed on 10 September 1959. It was withdrawn on 21 January 1961. Such was the success of these rebuilds that Sir Henry Fowler, Chief Mechanical Engineer from 1925 to 1931, built no fewer than 422 more locomotives of a similar design for the London, Midland & Scottish Railway. These appeared between 1924 and 1931. *ASF83-5 - Alec Swain*

Above: Newton Heath depot sees British Railways Standard Class 5 no. 73058 in residence on 10 September 1959. Or, rather, it was a visitor from 66A Polmadie in Glasgow. This build, from 1951 onwards, eventually totalled 172 locomotives, which were to be found all over the system. They did not, however, outlive last examples of the pre-war build of Stanier Class 5s, which lasted until the end of steam in 1968. No. 73058 was built in July 1954 and withdrawn from 61B Aberdeen in November 1964. *ASF84-4 - Alec Swain*

Below: A Class 108 DMU leaves Newton Heath station and passes the signal box. This has 22 steps to climb to gain entry, or for the signalman to dash down and place detonators on the line in an emergency. Having said that, the signalman might be able to get a much better idea of what is going on around him, which in itself is perhaps no bad thing. Of note is the shunting signal to the left of the box with four arms; such semaphores as remain today are mostly very ordinary. *ASF84-1 - Alec Swain*

Around Oldham

Below: Stanier Class 5 no. 44736 is hauling the 16:54 from Middleton Junction to Oldham Werneth up the very steep 1 in 27 of the half mile long Werneth Incline on 12 August 1953. It had only three coaches in tow, but this was quite enough! Originally a cable worked railway, matters improved with the arrival of diesel units, as long as the train concerned was of the two power cars variety, not one power and one trailer. Given the alternative route of the Oldham loop, the incline fell gradually into disuse, with final closure in 2009. *PH034 - Peter Hay*

Opposite Top: Oldham Central station had a very complete looking set of buildings on 14 April 1955, with a local train approaching bunker first from the Oldham Mumps direction. Although well sited for the town centre, the station was closed on 18 April 1966. It might be noted that Oldham once had five railway stations at Central, Clegg Street, Glodwick Road, Mumps and Werneth. These, and the lines that led to them, were owned by a number of different companies, either individually or jointly. *PY100111D - Henry Priestley*

Opposite Bottom: This Aspinall Class 27 no. 52466 of 26E was seen and photographed at Oldham Mumps Yard on 20 May 1960. There are a sizeable number of vacuum braked vans in the yard, seemingly of very modest size and hence capacity, but some of them will date back to when many road deliveries from railway yards were by horse and cart. It was their replacement by motor road vehicles which enabled delivery distances to be increased beyond that which a horse could (or might be persuaded to) go. *ASH82-1 - Alec Swain*

Above: Lees (Oldham) shed, 26F, is the home of both no. 49509 and no. 49662. Both were Fowler 7F 0-8-0s of 1929, though they were a development of the London & North Western Railway's G2s. The other locomotives have not been identified. There appears to have been a shed located in the vicinity since 1863, though the building seen here seems to have been built, or perhaps rebuilt, in 1955. It had five roads and there was also a turntable. It was closed finally on 16 May 1964, to be followed by that of the railway which passed it. *NS203973 - Neville Stead*

Opposite Top: The rail tour of 12 May 1956, which used Aspinall 3F no. 52438, included the Royton branch in its travels. This was a one mile long double track branch from Royton Junction, though somewhat curiously there was only one, decidedly lengthy, platform at the Royton terminus. It was opened on 21 March 1864. This was long enough to accommodate an eight coach train, so more than adequate for the diesel units which latterly provide the service. The locomotive of the special though had to run round its train and is being supervised here at Royton by at least seven visitors to the footplate plus sundry others. It is being coupled up to the coaches, the station time allowed at Royton being a total of 13 minutes. Branch passenger services ceased on 18 April 1966 and the station was closed. The branch station of Royton Junction on the Oldham loop was renamed Royton on 8 May 1978, but it too was closed on 11 May 1987. The nearby station of Derker was opened on 30 September 1985 and this provided an effective replacement. *AEB1192 - A. E. Bennett*

Opposite Bottom: Oldham Clegg Street looks decidedly deserted on 12 May 1956, the platform having but a single hand barrow on it. It is easily forgotten that such items have completely disappeared, together with the porters who used them. The Lancashire & Yorkshire 0-6-0 locomotive no. 52438 has arrived with the *Old Manchester Rail Tour* from Delph and is running round its train before setting off for Rochdale. Today, all rail services in Oldham are on what was the Oldham loop, as reconstructed in recent years, and are operated by Manchester Metrolink. National Railways have no part in this. *AEB1193 - A. E. Bennett*

Above: The nine mile branch from Rochdale to Bacup was completed in 1881. The line was intended primarily for goods traffic, but a passenger service was operated. It was closed to passengers on 16 June 1947, still in LMS days. This was said to be temporary and due to national coal shortages. But patronage was minimal, anyway, and the service was never restored. On 12 May 1956 the Stephenson and Manchester locomotive societies together promoted the Old Manchester Rail Tour, seen here at Facit, 5¾ miles from Rochdale, with no. 50647. *AEB1197 - A. E Bennett*

Opposite Top: Power for the Old Manchester Rail Tour's downhill run from Facit to Rochdale was provided by no. 50647, an Aspinall 2-4-2T of the Lancashire & Yorkshire Company, dating from 1889. Goods traffic on the branch had remained after passenger service withdrawal, but the line was gradually cut back. With punishing up gradients for the first seven miles of between 1 in 40 and 1 in 60 out of Rochdale, then a steep fall thereafter to Bacup, this was at best difficult territory. By 1967, it was closed and the track lifted. *AEB1196 - A. E. Bennett*

Opposite Bottom: Little used stations have never managed to offer more than basic facilities. New Hey station between Oldham and Rochdale, seen here in about 1962, would appear not to have much to offer. But then, what was it reasonable to expect? Bus stops will offer you a flag to indicate that this is an approved stopping place, and if you are lucky a timetable and some kind of shelter. The least you need from a railway station is a platform, lighting, and some means of crossing the line. Again, a timetable and shelter might be expected. The words on the huge building to the right reads LANCASHIRE AND YORKSHIRE RAILWAY COTTON WAREHOUSE. Today, the service provider here is Manchester Metrolink. *Photographer Unknown*

The Stanier 4-6-0 Class 5s and the 2-6-0 6P5Fs were remarkably similar in appearance. No. 42945 of 1933 is one of the latter, seen here at Rochdale on a passenger service. Rochdale was the terminating point for trains from Manchester via the Oldham loop line, but the Metrolink replacement service passes over the Network Rail line half a mile east of Rochdale station. It then stops outside the station and continues to its own terminal point in the town centre, a further half mile distant. Railway stations are not always known for their convenience of location. *FM24-5 - Larry Fullwood*

To Rochdale

Above: The versatile 'Black 5s' could go almost everywhere. Here no. 45105 hurries through the centre platform lines at Rochdale with a lengthy freight. To the right are some dowdy looking LNER coaches. The early British Railways express passenger stock livery of crimson lake with cream panels, lined with gold and black, was well on the way to wearing off. This colour scheme was known as 'blood and custard' to its detractors, who had a point. This would be replaced by lined maroon in 1957, which was decidedly more serviceable. *NS203999 - Neville Stead*

Below: Former London & North Eastern railway locomotives were often to be found in the Manchester area, particularly on line that crossed the Pennines. Here, Gresley Class V2 2-62 no. 60877 of 50A (York) is seen negotiating Rochdale's platforms with what appears to be a train of empty bogie bolster wagons. In 1952, British Railways owned an astonishing 1.1 million wagons of all descriptions but excluding service vehicles, of which very slightly over half were for the carriage of coal or other minerals. Private owner wagons were then very few, mostly relating to specialised traffics such as the transport of oil. *NS204151 - Neville Stead*

Clayton Bridge station was a typical Lancashire & Yorkshire wayside station of its period, having opened on the line between Manchester Victoria and Stalybridge on 13 April 1846. This view, looking east towards the signal box and level crossing was taken on 26 September 1964. This was before the railway reached Stalybridge (7 miles 63 chains from Manchester). *PY 10046C - Henry Priestley*

Top: The Stephenson and Manchester locomotive societies ran the *Whitby Moors Rail Tour* on 6 March 1965, shortly before the demise of many of the lines in the North Yorkshire area. Thus it would travel to stations such as Market Weighton, Filey Holiday Camp (1st reversal), Scarborough Londesborough Road (for the coastal branch), Ravenscar, Prospect Hill Junction (2nd reversal), Whitby Town (3rd reversal) and York. Jubilee 4-6-0 no. 45698 *Mars* is seen here doing the honours and arriving at Manchester Victoria with the empty stock. It will take the train forward at 09:30. *ASR46-2 - Alec Swain*

This is a rear view of the well spruced up Jubilee class 4-6-0 locomotive no. 45698 *Mars* as it enters Manchester Victoria with 1X15. This is the SLS/MLS *Whitby Moors Rail Tour* on 6 March 1965, running via Rochdale, Halifax and Cleckheaton to Wakefield Kirkgate, where there would be a change of engine. The train was 'topped and tailed' for the entire journey between Market Weighton and York, thus minimising reversal problems. The section from north of Prospect Hill Junction to Whitby West Cliff station and beyond had been closed in 1961, but incorporating this reversing move was the only way that trains from Scarborough could reach Whitby Town. It was, one might add, rather easier with a two-car dmu. That line was closed permanently two days later, on 8 March 1965. *FM24-5 - Larry Fullwood*

Opposite Top: The Hughes 'Crab' 2-6-0s were mixed traffic machines built between 1926 and 1932 to a substantial total of 245 locomotives. This is no. 42713, seen here on the Down Main line at Manchester Victoria on 28 August 1959, with the driver hoping to be able to keep going and not having to bring his passenger train to a stop for adverse signals. The photographer is standing on what was then the longest platform in Britain, at 2,258 ft. It was created by the LMS on 16 April 1929, linking Platform 11 at Victoria with Platform 3 at Exchange by inserting a Platform 11 middle. *ASF64-2 - Alec Swain*

Opposite Bottom: Fowler Patriot class 4-6-0 locomotive no. 45509 *The Derbyshire Yeomanry* was to haul train C801 out of Manchester Victoria's Platform 14 at 10:10 on 29 May 1960. This was a special for the Stephenson and Manchester locomotive societies, the *Northern Fells Rail Tour*, on 29 May 1960. The Patriot would take it to Lancaster Castle and thence Morecambe Promenade, arriving at 11:48. Participants would then travel, mostly behind no. 42952, via Lancaster Green Ayre to Glasson Dock, Wennington, Tebay, Kirby Stephen East, Arnside, Windermere Lakeside and back to Morecambe Promenade. No 45509 then brought the train back to Manchester. *NS203826 - Neville Stead*

Above: The General Post Office used trains on a large scale. With staff on board and while the train was on the move at speed, mail could be picked up by nets protruding from the vehicle side, or set down using traductor arms. Meanwhile, mail would be sorted into the appropriate bags. LMS Royal Mail van no. M30232M was photographed at Manchester Victoria; this had two sets of doors plus an area for the pick-up/set down apparatus. None of this precluded the train from stopping at stations to load and/or unload mail bags by the time-honoured method. There was also an external mail box, with flap, where anybody at a station could post late letters for an additional fee. *ASV82-6 - Alec Swain*

Stalybridge and Saddleworth

Above: This picture of Stalybridge platforms from 16 January 1962 indicates large, deserted premises. If the platforms look long that is because they were, with 11 or 12 coach capacities. Note, particularly, the two centre through lines, without platforms; today, only two lines continue east of the station, towards Diggle, though there is also on the right hand side of the formation, a bi-directional through line, the up Huddersfield. There was a fine four semaphore signal bracket to be seen here in the days before power signalling. There are now five platforms in total, two of which are bays. *PY10096S - Henry Priestley*

Below: In 1959's steam days, Stanier Class 5 4-6-0 no. 45095 is seen approaching Stalybridge from the Manchester direction, while a Metro-Cammell diesel unit, later Class 101, has got the road in the opposite direction. Today, a notable plus point about Stalybridge station is the Station Buffet Bar, entrance on Platform 4. This appears in the Good Beer Guide for 2022 and is on the Transpennine Real Ale Trail. Or, if you are enjoying yourself here, check out the Guide's comment that it is well worth missing a train. *NS208150 - Neville Stead*

Greenfield station is now the last remaining passenger station west of the Pennines on the London & North Western route via Standedge. No. 40014 was a 1930 4MT 2-6-2T built by H W Fowler and dating from 1930. It is seen here in the bay platform (now long gone) at Greenfield with a push-pull train to Oldham Clegg Street. Services on the Oldham – Greenfield - Delph axis ceased on 2 May 1955. *NS203816 - Neville Stead*

Opposite Top: The short branch from Greenfield to Delph was another target of the *Old Manchester Rail Tour*. The train is seen here at the Delph terminus on 12 May 1956 with Aspinall 0-6-0 no. 52438 in charge for this part of the journey. It would seem that virtually all of the train's passengers had disembarked. Closure to ordinary passenger traffic had taken place a year earlier on 2 May 1955. *AEB1194 - A. E. Bennett*

Opposite Bottom: Stanier Black 5 4-6-0 no. 45409 is crossing Upper Mill viaduct on the London & North Western route to Huddersfield and Leeds. Saddleworth station can be seen in the distance, but this was closed on 7 October 1968. Once, there was what amounted to a four tracked line over the 17 miles from Stalybridge to Huddersfield, but today a single passing loop on each line, at Diggle (eastbound) and Marsden (westbound), suffice. The track in the foreground is a small part of what once was there. The future sees a major upgrading as a distinct possibility, but will the Standedge tunnels be enlarged for the larger container traffic now on offer, which otherwise has to be routed via Carlisle and Newcastle? *NS203814 - Neville Stead*

Above: Towards the end of steam traction in 1968, the Stanier 'Black 5s' were about the only suitable steam locomotives left for hauling passenger trains. Here nos. 45079 and 45063 are double heading a train over Upper Mill viaduct across the River Tame in the course of their climbing into the Pennines to reach Diggle and the Standedge Tunnels. The latter are 3 miles 66 yards long, though there are a couple more, parallel but long disused tunnels, which might again conceivably be pressed into service while 'essential engineering work' takes place. *NS203815 - Neville Stead*

Manchester Ship Canal Railway

Above: The purpose of the Ship Canal was to reduce the time and cost of transporting goods between Manchester and Liverpool, and to circumvent the Port of Liverpool's handling charges, which were considered unreasonable. Hudswell Clarke, the builders, specialised in industrial tank engines, but nothing bigger than an 0-6-0T. This view shows Manchester Ship Canal (MSC) locomotive no. 35, an 0-6-0ST built by them and one of around 25. This is the version with short water tanks, which resulted in a locomotive with a well balanced look about it. Careful examination will reveal that the centre wheels are flangeless and the coupling rods hinged to allow some lateral movement. These were ruses to permit these locomotives to negotiate the very sharp curves which abounded on the system. *23491 - Photographer Unknown*

Opposite: MSC's no. 52 long tank 0-6-0ST is paired with a saloon which looks a little the worse for wear. Both are seen below the (relatively) vast bulk of the vessel *Pacific Stronghold*. It is 12 April 1959. This scene gives an idea of the amount of work needed to first excavate and then line such a huge trench in the ground, while also making provision in its width for ships to pass each other. It was for the use of the contractors that the initial railway was built and might have been dismantled soon afterwards. The operational canal railway that did emerge would, at its peak, own 230 miles of track, 75 locomotives and 2,700 wagons. It never became part of the nationalised system and was the largest private railway in the country. *RCR13160A - R. C. Riley*

Above: Another Hudswell Clarke product for MSC was 0-6-0ST no. 39 with a short tank. It is seen here shunting three Vanfits (covered vans each with vacuum brakes). A curiosity in this picture is the point in the foreground, or rather the remains of it. As it then stood it was clearly useless, but even so one would hardly expect to find a point lever for the adjoining track in the middle of the formation which would have led from it. Something, somewhere, was decidedly wrong, but perhaps it was decided that there was no future use for it and it could merely be abandoned. *23317 - Unknown Photographer*

Opposite Top: A much smaller locomotive was the Manchester Ship Canal's no. 78, Hudswell Clarke's works no 1584, an 0-6-0ST built in 1927. It lasted until 1972. This was a one off light weight saddle tank. It is seen here at Partington North, though not incredibly busy. When the Ship Canal railway finally converted wholly to diesels on 6 July 1976, it still owned in the order of 70 steam locomotives. *RCR13179 - R.C Riley*

Opposite Bottom: Dieselisation came to the Manchester Ship Canal company in the form of a pair of Hudswell Clarke 0-6-0 diesel electric locomotives in 1959, numbers 4001 and 4002. This is no. 4002, works no. D1076. Somewhat curiously, it was named *Arundel Castle*, the real version of which was 250 miles or so distant in West Sussex. Further diesels followed from a variety of manufacturers (these two came from Hudswell Clarke), but railway and indeed Ship Canal traffic levels were declining. The MSC railway line was subsequently closed finally to all traffic. *20441 - Unknown Photographer*

And Finally….

Above: A rail tour that took place on 21 May 1967 was that run by the Roch Valley Railway Society and the Locomotive Club of Great Britain. This covered the Trafford Park estates using ex-Lancashire & Yorkshire 0-4-0 saddle tank no. 51216, power category 0F, and a set of British Railways Goods Brake Vans. The locomotive weighed a mere 21 tons 5 cwt and was a remaining example of the class introduced in 1891 by Aspinall. By this stage it was no longer part of British Railways stock, being based in preservation at Haworth on the Keighley & Worth Valley Railway. It had been brought to Trafford Park for other duties, one of which was shunting at Brown & Polson cornflower works, as a temporary replacement for their own locomotive. *AS V85-1 - Alec Swain*

Opposite: In planning their railway works at Horwich, the Lancashire & Yorkshire Railway decided to build an 18in gauge internal transport system for moving components around. *Wren* was one of the eight locomotives designed for this job by Beyer Peacock and was built by them in 1887 - at a cost of £268. The substantial works railway system at Horwich was extended, eventually, to a length of 7½ miles. A secondary function of the narrow gauge railway was the distribution of wage packets, for which a strong box was added to the tender. This photograph is dated 19 March 1935. *Wren* continued in use until 1961, following which at the grand old age of 74 she was placed on static display within Horwich works. She now resides in the National Railway Museum at York for all to see, putting her age at well over 130 years. *GB215 - George Barlow*

Bibliography

Pre-Grouping Atlas and RCH Junction Diagrams. ISBN 978-0711038103. Ian Allan Ltd 2014.

Rail Atlas of Great Britain and Ireland. S K Baker. ISBN 978-0860936695 OPC 14th edition, 2015.

Railway Passenger Stations in England, Scotland and Wales: A Chronology (3rd edition) M E Quick. Railway & Canal Historical Society, 2005.

Railway Track Diagrams. Book 4: Midlands & North West. Martyn Brailsford for TRACK maps, 4th edition, December 2018.

The Railways of Great Britain, a Historical Atlas at a scale of 1 inch to 1 mile. Col. M H Cobb. ISBN 07110-3003-0, Ian Allan Publishers, 2003.

A Regional History of the Railways of Great Britain Volume 10 The North West. Geoffrey O Holt. ISBN 0946-537-34-8, David St John Thomas, 2nd edition, 1986.

The Railways of Manchester. C T Goode. ISBN 0-9508239-8-8, 1986.

The Last Steam Locomotives of British Railways. P Ransome-Wallis. Ian Allan Ltd 1966.

Various editions and titles of British Railways Locomotives, Ian Allan Ltd, also later Platform 5 Publishing.

British Railways timetables.

Wikipedia various, but especially in respect of individual locations, the informative Disused Stations Site Record, the Manchester Ship Canal and files giving details of past rail tours have proved most useful.